# MOTORCYCLES & MOTORCYCLING

# MOTORCYCLES & MOTORCYCLING

## BY MAX ALTH

FRANKLIN WATTS
NEW YORK | LONDON | TORONTO | 1979
A FIRST BOOK

Diagrams courtesy of Vantage Art, Inc.

Cover photograph courtesy of
*American Motorcyclist* magazine.

Interior photographs courtesy of: the New York
Public Library Picture Collection: pp. 3, 4, 8, 12, 15,
60 (top and bottom), 63 (top and bottom), 64 (top);
Butler & Smith, Inc./BMW: pp. 21, 44 (top and
bottom); American Motorcyclist Association: pp.
40, 73, 74, 77, 78, 83, 86; Kawasaki Motor Corp.:
pp. 45 (lower left), 53 (bottom); American Honda
Motor Corp.: pp. 45 (middle left), 50 (top), 51
(middle), 53 (top); Moto Guzzi Ltd.: pp. 45 (top
left, top right, middle right), 50 (bottom); Yamaha
Motor Corp.: p. 45 (bottom right); Max Alth: pp.
47, 57; Motobecane America Ltd.: pp. 50 (middle),
51 (top and bottom); Suzuki: p. 53 (middle);
National Archives: p. 63 (middle); U. S. Army: p.
64 (bottom left and bottom right).

Library of Congress Cataloging in Publication Data

Alth, Max, 1917–
    Motorcycles and motorcycling.

    (A First book)
    Bibliography: p.
    Includes index.
    SUMMARY: Explores the early history of bi-
cycles and motorcycles and the development of
modern-day motorcycles with a discussion of parts,
kinds of engines, and competitions.
    1. Motorcycles—Juvenile literature. 2. Motor-
cycling—Juvenile literature. [1. Motorcycles. 2.
Motorcycling] I. Title.
TL440.A46          629.22'75          79–12267
ISBN 0–531–02945–X

# CONTENTS

Dedicated to

Char
Misch
Mike
Syme
Arrabella
Mendle

and all other serious motorcycle fans

# CHAPTER ONE

# THE EARLY HISTORY OF MOTORCYCLES

Motorcycles have not been around a very long time. The first was built in 1865 by a man named Perreaux.

Perreaux' motorcycle was really a small steam engine attached to a bicycle frame. An oil burner was used to heat water in a boiler to make steam. The engine was connected with belts to the rear bicycle wheel.

As you can see, the first motorcycle was really part bicycle and part engine. The same is true of motorcycles today. Thus, to trace the development of the modern motorcycle, we must begin with a brief look at the development first of the bicycle, then of the engine.

## THE BICYCLE HALF
## OF THE MOTORCYCLE

The bicycle half of the motorcycle is almost two hundred years old. The first bicycle was made by a Frenchman named de Sivrac. It was just two wheels attached to a stick. In the spring of 1791, de Sivrac rode his invention down the garden paths of the Palais Royal in Paris. It looked like fun. Soon other people had bicycles. Eventually a group of bicyclists formed a club and raced their Celeriferes—as they called their bicycles—down the Champs Elysées, a large avenue in Paris. People called the bicyclists dandy riders. This was not a compliment.

But bicycling then wasn't really that much fun. Riders had to sit on a little pad in the middle of the stick. To move themselves forward, they had to push backward against the ground using their feet. The front wheel could not be steered. To make a turn, a rider had to push or pull the bicycle to one side. Very often the rider would injure a leg or stomach muscle while trying to make a fast turn.

**An 1813 model
Celerifere.**

**The "Draisienne"
of 1819.**

Twenty-six years later, in Germany, a man called the Baron von Drais was walking through a forest belonging to the Duke of Baden. He saw a man riding a Celerifere. He tried to ride it himself. He didn't like it. He got off, looked at the bicycle, and decided to change the front wheel so that the vehicle could be steered from side to side. This meant there was no longer much danger of the rider getting hurt while going around a corner. He also added an armrest. From then on the Baron rode everywhere on his "Draisienne."

The bicycle was now a useful item. A person can walk 4 miles (6.4 km) per hour and average 20 miles (32 km) a day. On the Draisienne, which weighed about 55 pounds (25 kg), a person could go 9 miles (14.5 km) per hour and average 50 miles (80 km) a day. Even a horse and rider could not keep up this pace for more than a few days.

Although in 1817 a Draisienne cost as much as a small motorcycle costs today, thousands of them were made and sold.

But the bicycle still remained a joke. People called it by many humorous names. They called it boneshaker, swift walker, dandy horse, even hobby horse. They made fun of bicycle riders. The newspapers of that time often published cartoons that depicted bicyclists as appearing very foolish and clumsy to amused onlookers.

Most people soon lost interest in bicycles. But the inventors did not. They made all kinds of strange new contraptions. Some had two wheels. Others—tricycles—had three wheels. Still others had four wheels, while the unicycle had only one wheel. One unicycle had a wheel so big that the rider sat at its midpoint while the wheel rolled around the person.

But basically they were all the same. The rider's feet still had to touch the ground. The rider still had to push backward to move forward. The only time the rider could ride with feet off the ground was while coasting down a hill.

Twenty years passed. The boneshaker remained a walking machine. Then, in 1839 in Scotland, a man named Kirkpatrick Macmillan built the first real or true bicycle. He connected levers and pedals to the rear wheel. With these his bicycle could reach a speed of 14 miles (22.5 km) per hour. The rider's feet didn't have to touch the ground anymore. The rider could turn right or left more easily. But no one was interested. Few bicycles were built.

Then, in 1861, a Frenchman named Pierre Michaux changed all that. Michaux repaired wagons and coaches for a living. He had a helper named Pierre Lallement. (We will hear more of Lallement later.) One day a boneshaker was brought to the Michaux shop in Paris. Michaux not only fixed it, he also added a crank to its front wheel. Now the rider could turn the front wheel directly with his or her feet. No more levers, no more pushing on the ground.

Suddenly everyone wanted a Michaux bicycle with a front-wheel pedal. Michaux put his family and Lallement to work. They made 400 pedal boneshakers a year. By 1885, there were 400,000 of them on the roads of England alone.

The pedals on the Michaux bicycle were fastened directly to the front wheel. Every time the pedals went around once, the front wheel went around once. The larger the front wheel, the farther it would go each time it was turned and the faster the bicycle would go. Thus, the size of the front wheel kept getting larger and larger until it reached 5 feet (1.5 m) in diameter. This was as far as a tall person's legs could reach. As the front wheel got larger, the rear wheel got smaller. The rider sat 6 feet (1.8 m) above the ground.

The name of the bicycle was changed at this time from the boneshaker to the ordinary and penny farthing. No one remembers why. But the high-wheel ordinary was much more dangerous than the boneshaker. On the boneshaker, a rider could injure a leg or stomach muscle. On the ordinary, a rider could get killed. Hitting a bump while going downhill or running into a startled chicken could cause the rider to go sailing through the air. Many riders broke their necks this way. Some just cracked their skulls as they hit the ground.

The long spokes on the ordinary were also dangerous. There were so many of them, and they were so long, that it was easy to catch one's foot in them. To prevent this, riders always raised their feet clear of the pedals as they coasted down hills.

Hundreds of bicycle riders were killing or injuring themselves every year. The need for a safer bicycle soon became apparent, and was filled by H. J. Lawson of Britain in 1879. Lawson moved the pedals from the wheel to the middle of the bicycle. Then he attached a large gear wheel to the pedals. Next, he attached a small gear wheel to the rear wheel. Finally, he connected the two gear wheels together with a chain.

On Lawson's safety bicycle, when the rider worked the pedals, the front gear wheel would turn, which would then turn the rear gear wheel and the rear wheel. If both gear wheels were the same size, both would turn at the same speed. But if one were larger than the other, the smaller would turn faster. This made it unnecessary to have a giant front wheel. You could get the same speed by using a large front gear wheel.

For some unknown reason, the public did not take to the safety bicycles right away. For years the giant-wheel ordinaries continued to be manufactured and ridden. It was not until

**Some high-wheel ordinaries
of the early 1800s.**

1892 that the last ordinary was made and sold. By this time, more than a million people were riding bicycles of one kind or another.

## RIDING ON AIR

Up until this time, bicycle wheels had been made of wood or metal. The rims on the wheels had also been made of wood at first. Later, iron replaced the wood, and still later bicycles had hard or solid rubber tires on top of metal rims. Solid rubber has very little bounce. Riding a bicycle that had solid tires wasn't much more comfortable than riding one that had metal rims alone.

Then in 1888 an Irish veterinary surgeon named John Boyd Dunlop found a way of making a hollow tube of rubber and sealing air inside, thus inventing the air tire. Dunlop's tire, called the pneumatic tire, had a lot of bounce. It made the bicycle and many other vehicles more comfortable to ride.

The modern bicycle had arrived. From that time until now, there have been no major changes in the bicycle. Today, we ride almost the same bicycle people rode in 1900.

But what about the other half of the motorcycle—the engine?

## FIRST THERE
## WAS STEAM

Bicycles are considered to be human-propelled vehicles. They run on human energy. Automobiles, trucks, and motorcycles are considered to be self-propelled vehicles. By virtue of fuel and engines, they propel themselves. The first self-propelled vehicle in history was a three-wheel steam-engine-powered wagon built by a man named N. J. Cugnot for the French army in 1796. This wagon had a huge copper ball filled with water, a stove that turned the water to steam, and a steam engine. All these parts were fastened above a huge single front wheel. Most likely the steam wagon did not work too well. A second steam wagon was never constructed.

Five years later, in Britain, a man named Richard Trevithic built the first steam engine ever to pull passenger cars over rails. Steam engines were not new, but until Trevithic all steam engines were as big as a house. They worked very slowly and had very little power for their size and weight. The Trevithic engine was much smaller and lighter. It used only a small amount of steam at high pressure.

Once Trevithic showed the way, lots of other inventors followed. Steam engines became even smaller, lighter, and stronger. Inventors began installing them in three-wheel carriages and on the frames of tricycles. By 1850, there were thousands of steam-driven tricycles in Europe alone.

## EARLY MOTORCYCLES

The first person to try powering a bicycle with a steam engine was Perreaux in 1865, as mentioned earlier. The first American motorcycle was made by a man named Silvester Roper in 1868. Roper also used a steam engine. He placed the engine near the rear wheel of a Michaux bicycle and connected it to the wheel with rods. To make the steam needed to drive the engine, he used a small boiler heated by a coal fire. It must have been hot riding Roper's motorcycle. The boiler was placed under the seat.

Hot or not, his motorcycle worked. Roper made ten of them. He might have made more, but on a hot June day in 1896 he had a heart attack and died. He had been in the act of demonstrating his steam bicycle at the Charles River Bicycle (Racing) Track in Cambridge, Massachusetts.

How did Roper, an American, come to be using a Michaux bicycle for the body of his motorcycle? Pierre Lallement, mentioned earlier as Michaux' helper, had taken it to America claiming *he* had invented it and that Michaux had stolen the design from *him.*

Lucius Copeland of Phoenix, Arizona, was another early American motorcycle inventor. Copeland first tried to power a high-wheel ordinary using a small steam engine that was available at the time. However the engine was too big and heavy for the bicycle. Copeland then spent three years building his own engine. When he completed it in 1884, it weighed only 18 pounds (8.2 kg), including the boiler. Copeland mounted the engine and boiler on the front of a high-wheeler and then connected the engine to the big wheel with a belt.

This light, high-power engine made Copeland's motorcycle practical. On level ground it could reach a speed of 12 miles (19.3 km) per hour.

In 1887, Copeland formed the Northrop Manufacturing Company of New Jersey. Within three months, his company was producing for sale reliable steam-powered tricycles he called Phaeton Moto-Cycles. This was followed by production of a two-seater steam-powered motorcycle in 1888. Later, a small third wheel was added to the side of the motorcycle to keep it from tipping over when standing motionless. And later still, a third seat was added to the arm that held the third wheel. Thus the motorcycle sidecar was born.

By 1890, Northrop Manufacturing claimed it had made and

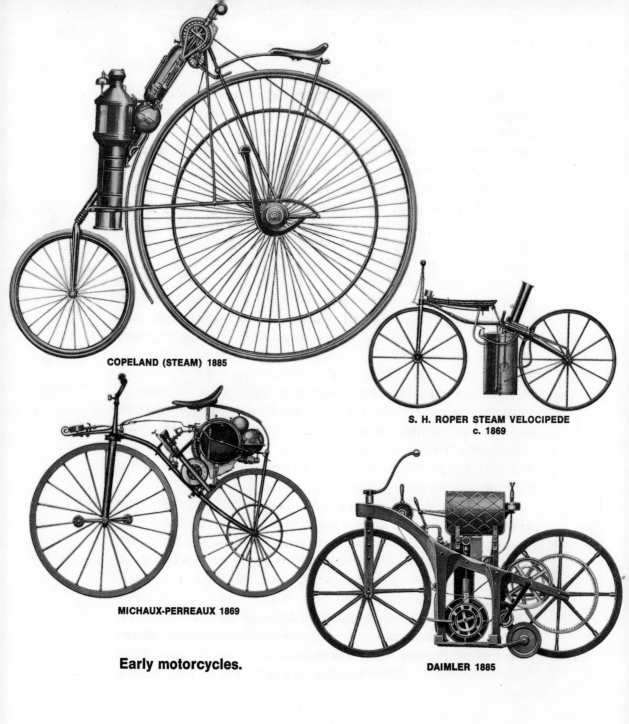

COPELAND (STEAM) 1885

S. H. ROPER STEAM VELOCIPEDE
c. 1869

MICHAUX-PERREAUX 1869

**Early motorcycles.**

DAIMLER 1885

sold more than two hundred of its machines. Each Moto-Cycle could go 30 miles (48 km) before it had to stop to take on water for its engine and could average a speed of 10 miles (16 km) per hour over this distance. However, top speed was probably little more than 15 miles (24 km) per hour, and on a cold morning it could take five minutes to bring the water to a boil and get going.

## ENTER THE INTERNAL-COMBUSTION ENGINE

A steam engine is an *external*-combustion engine. The combustion, or burning of the fuel, takes place *outside* the engine. Gasoline and diesel engines are *internal*-combustion engines. In these, the combustion of the fuel takes place *inside* the engine.

The first motorcycle to be powered by an internal-combustion engine was made in Germany in 1885 by Gottlieb Daimler and his associate, Wilhelm Mayback. The two men first mounted a gasoline engine inside the frame of an ancient wooden bicycle. They then placed two small wheels at the sides of the bicycle to keep it from falling over.

The experiment worked, but it was not followed up with mass production. We don't know why. We do know that Daimler later went into partnership with a man named Benz. Together the two built automobiles. Their company was a great success and still builds automobiles today—the Mercedes-Benz.

At about the same time, Edward Butler constructed a remarkable tricycle in Britain. It was remarkable in that it was powered by the most advanced gasoline engine of its time. The engine in Butler's machine was the first to use electric ignition. Before this, fuel inside the engine had to be ignited by means of a small flame.

The Butler machine ran very well, but it didn't sell very well. The reason for this was probably Britain's Locomotive Act, a law in effect at the time that made it illegal to drive a self-propelled vehicle at a speed of more than 4 miles (6.4 km) per hour. A person can walk all day at a speed of 4 miles (6.4 km) per hour and can run five times faster for a short distance. A horse can run at a speed of more than 40 miles (64 km) per hour for a mile (1.6 km) or more.

The Locomotive Act was originally passed mainly to protect the railway industry from competition with motorcycles and horseless carriages (motor-cars). It was not repealed until 1896.

In 1896, the average person's concept of speed was somewhat limited. Many times a British constable (policeman) would catch a speeder by running after the person on foot. When the speeding motorcyclist or horseless-carriage driver would come before the judge, the constable would say the speeder had been going 40 or more miles (64 km) per hour.

Between the years 1885 and 1900, hundreds of inventors and mechanics worked at improving the motorcycle. Their motorcycles worked, but not too well. Many small factories opened, made a few motorcycles which they couldn't sell, and promptly went out of business.

The first commercially successful motorcycle was made by a group of engineers in Munich, Germany. Heinrich and Wilhelm Hildebrand, Alois Wolfmuller, and Hans Greisenhof began their work together in 1892 by attaching steam engines to bicycles. Then they substituted a gasoline engine for the steam engine. But it wasn't until they made a frame especially suited to their engine that they were able to make a practical

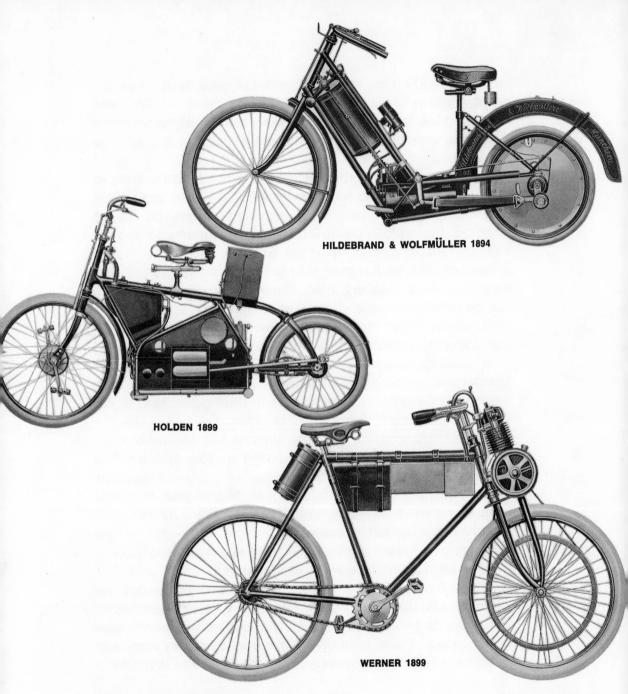

HILDEBRAND & WOLFMÜLLER 1894

HOLDEN 1899

WERNER 1899

**More early motorcycles.**

motorcycle. Their machine weighed 115 pounds (52 kg) and could reach a speed of 24 miles (39 km) per hour. This was just about the fastest any motorcycle could go at the time and it became very popular. At one time their company employed twelve hundred people.

Colonel H. Capel Holden in Britain followed the Germans' lead. He too used a frame made especially for his motorcycle rather than simply attaching an engine to a bicycle. Holden patented his motorcycle in 1894 and manufactured it from 1897 to 1902. It differed from the German motorcycle in that it had a four-cylinder engine in place of a two-cylinder engine (see next chapter). Also, the Holden engine was connected directly to the rear wheel of the motorcycle.

In France, where the bicycle was invented, the de Dion-Bouton Company manufactured a motorcycle in 1899 consisting of a standard bicycle powered by a small gasoline engine. The engine drove the rear wheel by means of a belt. Although the Dion-Bouton motorcycle did not go as fast as the German motorcycle, it cost a lot less and so became popular.

At the same time two brothers, Eugene and Michel Werner, manufactured a motorcycle they called a motorcyclette. The motorcyclette was a standard bicycle with a small gasoline engine mounted above its front wheel. The engine drove the front wheel by means of a belt. The bike's pedals were not disconnected but left in place. This made it possible for the driver to pedal the machine when the motor needed help or when the driver did not want to use the motor.

Almost the exact same arrangement of parts and engine position are still used today on the Solex, a moped (see Chapter Three) made by Motobecane. Only a belt drive is no longer used. Instead, the engine drives the front wheel by means of a rubber wheel that presses against the front tire. Millions of these machines have been manufactured and are in use all over the world today.

Just a few years later (the exact date is not known but it was probably 1903), the first true motorcycle appeared. It was the James, constructed by the James Cycle Co. of Britain. The James had a powerful Belgian engine mounted within a loop frame—no pedals, just a drive belt from the engine to the rear wheel. This machine had no bicycle parts. It was all motorcycle.

Within just a year or so of this, inventors and engineers succeeded in vastly improving the gasoline engine. They made it more powerful and faster. By 1904, the James and the Indian (an American motorcycle) could go 50 miles (80 km) per hour.

The modern motorcycle had arrived. It was safe, fast, light, and dependable. In the years that followed, the motorcycle would be further improved. But it would not really be changed ever again. Motorcycles today look a lot different than the motorcycles of 1904. But they are not a great deal different. They are just better.

# CHAPTER TWO

# HOW MOTORCYCLES WORK

All motorcycles have two wheels and a frame to hold the wheels in line, just like a bicycle. All motorcycles also have an engine of one kind or another to turn the rear wheel and make the motorcycle go forward.

The **front wheel** of the motorcycle spins on an axle, or shaft, that is held by a fork-like piece of metal. The top of this metal structure fits into a tube at the front end of the motorcycle **frame** and is attached to the **handlebars.** The motorcycle driver sits on a **seat** on top of the frame. Usually, his or her feet rest on **supports** attached to both sides of the frame, near its bottom.

To start the motorcycle, the operator inserts a key into the **ignition** and turns it. This switches the **engine** on. To drive the motorcycle, the operator must work the various **controls.** These controls are explained in detail a little further on. At very low speeds, the motorcycle is steered by turning the handlebars to the right or left. This turns the front wheel from side to side. Usually the driver also leans a little to the side he or she is turning to. At higher speeds, steering is accomplished almost entirely by leaning.

The **rear wheel,** like the front wheel, is mounted on an axle. It is free to spin, but unlike the front wheel it cannot turn from side to side.

To increase speed, the operator of a motorcycle turns the **throttle** on the handlebar. Doing so gives the engine more fuel and causes it to speed up. To reduce speed, the driver releases the throttle. The engine will then receive less fuel and thus slow down. To stop, the driver uses the **brakes.** To park the motorcycle, the driver shuts off the ignition and pushes the motorcycle up on its **stand** or uses its side stand.

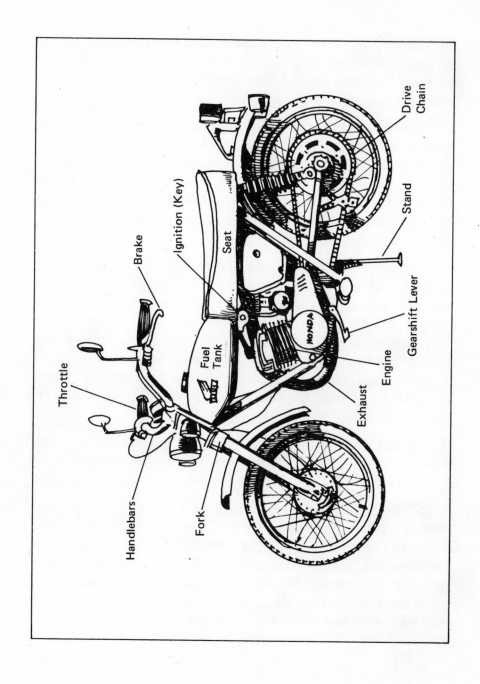

**The motorcyclist on this BMW is making a sharp turn, which he accomplishes almost entirely by leaning.**

## WHAT HOLDS THE MOTORCYCLE UP

If you have ever played with a toy gyroscope, you know that once its wheel is rapidly spinning, the gyroscope will stay in motion quite a long time. It will hold any position you place it in, too. When its wheel finally does stop turning, the gyroscope tilts and falls to one side.

The force that holds the gyroscope in position when its wheel is spinning is called gyroscopic force. The scientific principles explaining gyroscopic force were first stated by the great physicist Sir Isaac Newton. Newton said that a body in motion tends to stay in motion (until opposing forces stop it) and that a body moving in a circular motion tends to hold its position as well.

Because of this, a bicycle or motorcycle will stay up as long as its wheels are kept spinning.

The more rapidly a wheel spins and the heavier the wheel, the stronger the gyroscopic force. The gyroscopic force that results when a large, heavy wheel is spun rapidly is so great, in fact, that large gyroscopes are used to keep ocean liners steady during storms.

## POWER

All kinds of engines can and have been used to power motorcycles: electric motors; steam and piston engines fueled by gasoline, oil, or propane; rotary (Wankle) engines; rocket engines; even giant springs that were wound up with a giant key, like you wind up an alarm clock.

Today, the gasoline-fueled piston engine, which works exactly like the engine used in most cars, is used to power almost all motorcycles. Except for a few experimental models, all other motorcycles have electric motors powered by batteries.

## Steam Engines

Although steam engines are no longer used on motorcycles, a review of how they work will make the gasoline engine easier to understand.

A small steam engine will have a single **cylinder** and a single **piston.** A cylinder is a short tube. A piston is a kind of long plug that fits inside the cylinder and is free to move up and down in it. The piston is connected to a **crankshaft** by a rod. Every time the piston moves up and down in the cylinder, the crankshaft turns once.

One end of the cylinder is open. This is the end where the piston goes. The other end of the cylinder is closed except for two **valves.** Valves are used to control the flow of liquids and gases. A faucet is a kind of valve. Open it and water flows out. Close it and the water stops flowing.

One of the two valves in the closed end of the cylinder leads to the open air. The second is connected to a pipe that leads to a boiler partially filled with water.

The water is heated, causing it to boil and turn to steam. The steam has nowhere to go but through the pipe and into the cylinder. Since the steam is under pressure—water expands a thousand times when it turns to steam—it pushes out with force in all directions. The only thing the steam can move is the piston. When the steam presses against the piston, the piston is moved down toward the open end of the cylinder. As the piston moves, it turns the crankshaft. When the piston has moved as far down the cylinder as it can go, the valve

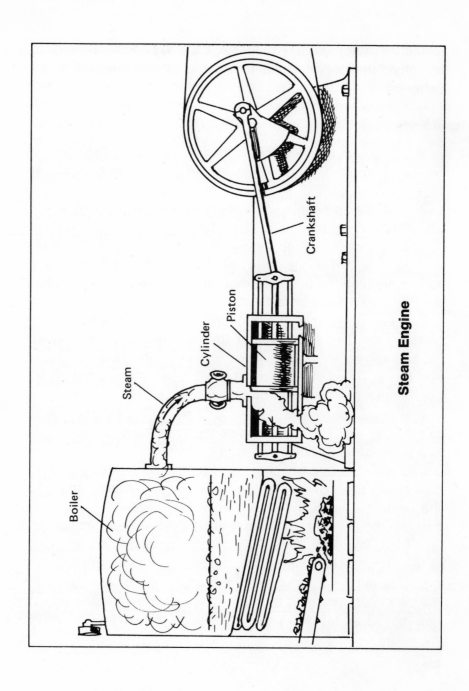

Crankshaft

Piston

Cylinder

Steam

Boiler

**Steam Engine**

leading to the steam is closed. The other valve leading to the air is opened. The steam within the cylinder escapes.

Once the crankshaft has been set in motion, it will continue turning for a short while. In that time it will move the piston all the way back up the cylinder. When the piston has gone as far as it can, the valve to the air is automatically closed. The valve connected to the steam is automatically opened. Steam again enters the cylinder and again pushes the piston toward the other end of the cylinder.

And so it goes. Steam enters the cylinder, pushes the piston, and then escapes. As the steam leaves it snorts. You may have heard large steam engines in railway trains do this when they start moving their load.

## Gasoline Engines

A gasoline engine operates much like a steam engine. It has a cylinder with a piston attached to a crankshaft and valves in the top of the cylinder. But, in addition, a gasoline engine has a **spark plug** positioned at the closed end of its cylinder. We'll talk more about the spark plug later.

The power to move the piston in the steam engine was supplied by the steam, which expanded inside the cylinder and pressed against the top of the piston.

The power to move the piston in a gasoline engine is supplied by a mixture of gasoline and air, which is ignited and burned right inside the cylinder.

Steam engines are self-starting. To get a steam engine going, you merely let steam into the cylinder. Gasoline engines must be started up. This means the driver must turn the engine's crankshaft him- or herself (or have an electric motor do it) so that the piston will move up and down within the cylinder and suck in the needed fuel-air mixture.

25)

There are two kinds of gasoline piston engines. One is called a **four-cycle** or **four-stroke**—also sometimes called an Otto-cycle after its inventor, N. A. Otto, who patented it in 1876. The other is called a **two-stroke.** Dugald Clerk, the man who invented and patented the two-stroke in 1881 is all but forgotten.

The four-stroke engine produces smoother power, makes a less irritating noise, and lasts longer. However the two-stroke produces more power per pound (kg) of engine weight than the four-stroke. The two-stroke is also a little less expensive to manufacture. It has fewer parts.

Since the four-stroke engine is easier to understand, we'll look at that one first. Once you understand how the four-stroke operates, it is only a simple jump to understanding the two-stroke.

**Four-stroke engines.** To see how they work, let's look at one in the process of operating. The engine is turned on. At the instant we look at it, the piston is up near the top of the cylinder and moving down. The cylinder's **intake valve,** leading to the **carburetor,** is open. (The carburetor is the place where the fuel and air are mixed.) The cylinder's **exhaust valve,** which leads to the open air, is closed. As the piston moves down, the cylinder sucks in the mixture of fuel and air. This is the initial movement and is called the intake stroke.

When the piston reaches the bottom of the cylinder and starts back up, the intake valve is closed. The exhaust valve remains closed. As the piston moves upward toward the closed end of the cylinder, the fuel-air mixture is compressed. This is called the second or compression stroke.

When the piston is at the top of its stroke, close to the valves and spark plug, the plug is fired. That is, high voltage electricity is made to jump across the spark plug's gap

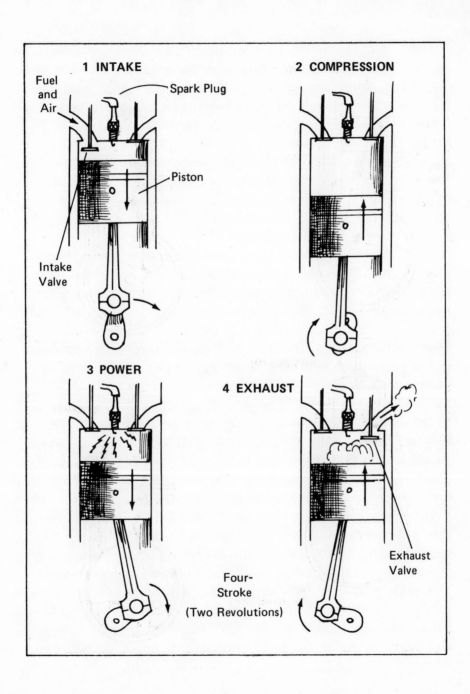

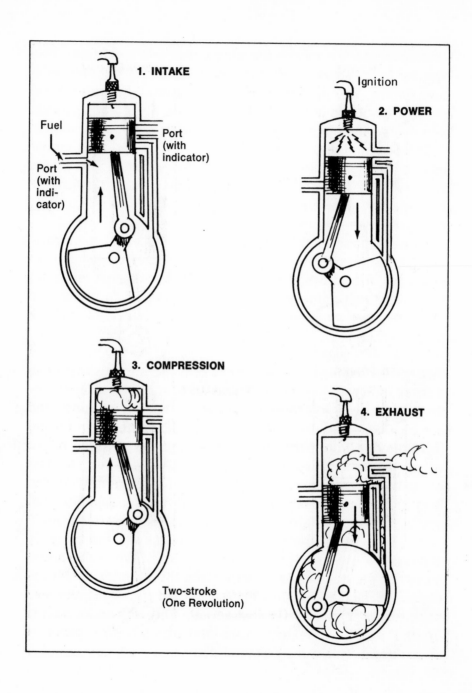

1. INTAKE

Fuel

Port
(with
indicator)

Port
(with
indi-
cator)

Ignition

2. POWER

3. COMPRESSION

4. EXHAUST

Two-stroke
(One Revolution)

(the open space between the plug's side and electrode). This results in a spark, and the spark sets the fuel-air mixture on fire. The mixture burns very rapidly. (It does *not* explode, though, as is usually thought.) The heated air expands and pushes the piston down. This is the third or power stroke.

The piston moves down as far as it can go and then moves upward again. The exhaust valve is now opened. The intake valve remains closed. As the piston moves up, it pushes the burned gas mixture out of the cylinder. This is the fourth or exhaust stroke. It is the final stroke.

When all four strokes are completed, the exhaust valve is closed, the intake valve is opened again, and the engine repeats the four strokes just described, and keeps repeating them until the engine is shut off. The driver shuts the engine off by simply switching off the flow of electricity to the spark plug.

**Two-stroke engines.** Each cylinder of a two-stroke engine has a spark plug and four **ports.** These ports serve the same function as valves in the four-stroke but are slightly different and are positioned on the side of the cylinder rather than on the top. Like the four-stroke engine, one port works as an intake valve. The second works as an exhaust valve. The other two are called **transfer ports.** They connect to each other and also lead to the **crankcase.** The crankcase is a metal box that encloses the bottom end of the cylinder and the crankshaft.

In a two-stroke, the piston opens and closes the ports by sliding over them as it moves up and down. When the piston moves down, it sucks fuel and air into the cylinder. When the piston moves up, it pushes the old burned gases out and also compresses the unburned fuel and air. Then the spark plug is fired. The fuel-air mixture burns and expands. The piston is driven down. This is the power stroke.

If you remember, only one stroke out of four was a power stroke in a four-stroke engine. In a two-stroke, every second stroke is a power stroke.

## RPM

A piston engine can have any number of cylinders (and pistons). But whether an engine has one, two, four, or more cylinders, all the pistons are attached to a single crankshaft. As the pistons move up and down inside their cylinders, they turn the crankshaft.

The faster the pistons move, the more rapidly the crankshaft turns. Crankshaft speed is measured in revolutions per minute (rpm). Since the crankshaft is connected to the rear wheel of the motorcycle, the faster the crankshaft "turns over," the faster the motorcycle will go.

The crankshaft on the average motorcycle engine turns over at about 5,000 rpm. Auto-racing engines can rotate more than 12,000 rpm. If a piston engine turns over too rapidly, it will sometimes literally fly apart. That is what is meant by an engine throwing a connecting rod or blowing its head.

The average motorcycle-engine crankshaft rotates about 15,000 to 25,000 times for each mile (1.6 km) the motorcycle travels. As you can see, engines are pretty busy when they are running.

## ENGINE DISPLACEMENT

One way engine power is measured is by the volume of space displaced by the piston in its movement from the bottom to the top of the cylinder. This amount is called an engine's displacement and is usually measured in cubic centimeters (cc). Since all the pistons in an engine work together, the cc of all the cylinders are added together to find the total displacement of an engine.

Almost all manufacturers of gasoline piston engines list the engine displacement number as the major engine specification. Many motorcycle manufacturers even make the engine displacement number a part of their motorcycle's name—the Honda 250, the Suzuki 75, and so on. The reason for doing this is that these numbers are a quick way for a buyer to know how large an engine is. Generally, you can assume that engine displacement is a good indication of engine power. A 200-cc engine produces about twice as much power as a 100-cc engine, for example.

Moped motorcycles have engines with displacements of 50 cc or less. True motorcycles have engines with displacements ranging from 75 to 1,200 cc. So far, no mass-production motorcycle engine has been built with more than six cylinders, although Moto-Guzzi, an Italian manufacturer, did build some eight-cylinder models to be used mostly for Grand Prix racing.

Small cars have engines that range from 1,000 to 2,000 cc. Large cars have engines that run to more than 5,000 cc. Modern cars have engines with four, five, six, and eight cylinders.

## POWER TRAIN

One wheel on a motorcycle is always connected to the crankshaft. This is usually the back wheel. Whatever is used to connect the crankshaft of an engine to a motorcycle's wheel is called a **power train.** Some power trains are really simple devices.

31)

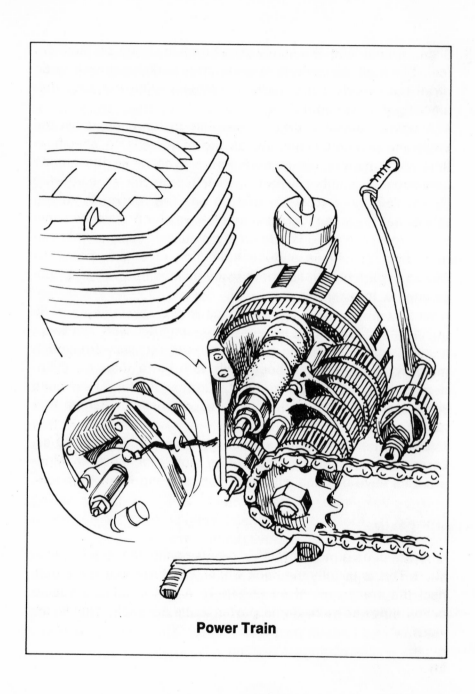

**Power Train**

The first motorcycle makers used belts to connect their engines to their motorcycle wheels. This method is still used on many mopeds. Other early motorcycle makers used a rubber wheel on the end of the crankshaft as their power train. The rubber wheel pressed down on the motorcycle's tire. When the engine turned over, the wheel turned. This method is also still used on some mopeds.

But today most motorcycle power trains are more complicated. They consist of a **clutch,** a **gearbox,** and one or two **chains.** Each part has a special purpose.

### Clutch

The clutch is used to separate the engine from the rest of the power train. If the engine is not separated from the power train, it will shut down every time the motorcycle stops moving. The clutch lets the driver disconnect the motor but leave it running when he or she wants to stop the motorcycle temporarily, such as for a red light.

**Wet clutch.** Almost all motorcycles use "wet" clutches in their power trains. These consist of two groups of metal plates that rotate in a pool of oil. (The plates are wet with oil, not water.) One group of plates is connected to the engine. The other group of plates is connected to the rest of the power train.

When the motorcycle is rolling along, a heavy spring presses all the plates together. This causes the engine to turn the power train and move the motorcycle.

When the driver wants to disconnect—called disengage—the motor from its power train, he or she presses the **clutch control lever** against the handlebars. Doing so moves a lever in the clutch. The lever pushes the spring back. The plates are now free to slide past one another. The motorcycle stops, but the engine continues running.

**33)**

## Gears

Minibikes and mopeds, which are both very small motorcycles, rarely have gears between their clutch and rear wheel. All other motorcycles do. Gears are used to regulate speed. For example, if the crankshaft of an engine is rotating at 3,000 rpm and you want the rear wheel to rotate at 300 rpm, you would use the gears to make it happen.

Gears work like this: All gear wheels have teeth. When the teeth on one gear wheel are meshed with the teeth on a second gear wheel, they are locked together. You will get an idea of how this works by placing the fingers of one hand between the fingers of your other hand. Note how your hands are actually locked—meshed—together in this position.

If two gear wheels are meshed, when one turns the other must turn also. If both gear wheels have the same number of teeth, they will turn at the same speed. But if the first wheel has, say, ten teeth, and the second has twenty teeth, the second wheel will turn only half as fast as the first wheel. If the first wheel has five teeth and the second wheel has fifty teeth, the second wheel will turn one-tenth as fast as the first. The small wheel has to turn around ten times to make the big wheel turn around once.

In this way, it is possible to make an engine crankshaft that rotates at 3,000 rpm turn a motorcycle wheel at only 300 rpm. At this gear ratio—ten to one—the average motorcycle would be moving at about 20 miles (32 km) per hour.

When you want to get a motorcycle moving from a standing-still position, you want the rear wheel to turn at a very slow speed at first. Once the motorcycle is moving, you will probably want the rear wheel to turn a little faster. Later, you may want the rear wheel to turn faster still.

Some speed change can be made with the throttle. The

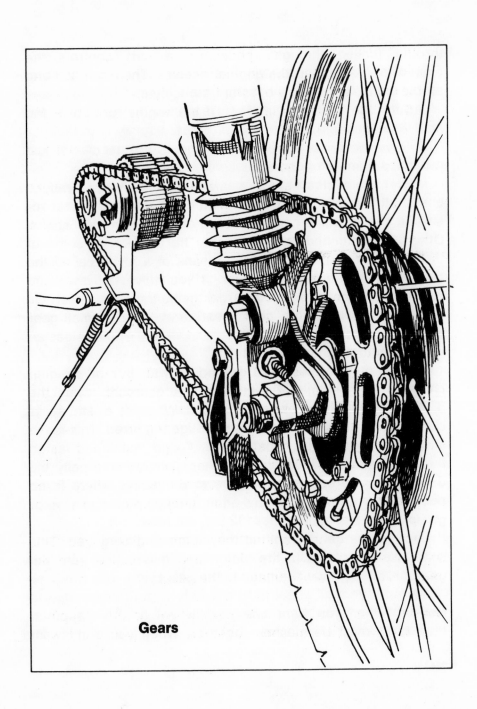

**Gears**

throttle (called the gas pedal on a car) controls the amount of fuel and air the engine receives. The more fuel and air the engine receives, the faster it turns over.

But throttle control is limited. If the engine turns over too fast, it can damage itself.

To give the driver speed control, gears are used—not just two, but a number of gears.

Most motorcycles have a gearbox (which is not really a box at all!). This gearbox contains a number of gears that rotate on shafts. Some can slide back and forth on their shafts. Others are attached to the clutch. The position of some of these gears can be changed by means of a lever, called the **gear lever** or the **gearshift lever.** If you move the lever and cause a little gear to turn a larger gear, the rear wheel will turn more slowly. If you "shift" gears and cause a small gear to turn another small gear, the rear wheel will turn faster, and the motorcycle will go faster.

Modern motorcycles have gearboxes with five or six gear changes or positions. By moving the gearshift lever, the driver can select the gear ratio wanted. When he or she starts out or has to go up a steep hill, "first" gear is used. This is the slowest speed and the most power. To go faster and faster, the driver shifts to higher and higher gear ratios. Finally the driver is at top speed and may just roll along. There is no need to change or shift gears again until it is time to stop or go up a very steep hill.

Each time a gear is shifted the clutch is disengaged. This separates the plates in the clutch and the engine from the gearbox, all to prevent damage to the gears.

**Neutral.** When you want one gear wheel to drive another, their teeth must be meshed together. When you don't want this to happen, but you want to leave the engine running, you separate the gear wheels by moving the gear lever to the **neutral** position. The engine will continue to turn over, but the motorcycle will stand still.

### Drive Chain

Most motorcycle engines are placed in the middle of the motorcycle. The clutch is next to the engine and the gearbox is right next to the clutch. The rear wheel is a foot or two (.3 or .6 m) away. The **drive chain** is used to connect the gear-box to the rear wheel.

Some motorcycles use a **drive shaft** in place of a drive chain. The trouble with the drive chain is that it is exposed and greasy. The driver can easily get his or her clothing dirty. Also, a drive chain requires more maintenance than a drive shaft.

The drive shaft is a rod that turns. One end is connected to the gearbox. The other end has a bevel gear. This is a gear that works sideways. It turns a gear on the rear wheel.

### OPERATING THE CONTROLS

Let us say that you are old enough to drive and want to learn how to operate a motorcycle. You have just purchased one and are about to go for your first ride on it. What do you do?

First, you move your motorcycle, or bike, as most riders prefer to call their machines, up on its **kickstand.** The bike can now stand by itself. It will not fall over.

You open the fuel valve and move the gear lever to neutral. The **choke** is moved to its closed position. This reduces the air that goes into the carburetor but not the gasoline, thus making the mixture more rich in gasoline than it needs to be for normal running. You turn the ignition key. This provides the electricity the spark plug needs to fire.

Next, you step down hard on the **kick-start pedal.** (Many motorcycles today have **electric starters** instead of kick-start pedals.) As the engine coughs into life, you twist the right handlebar grip. This is the throttle. Turning it counterclockwise lets more gas and air into the engine. The engine speeds up. For the next minute or so you hold the throttle steady. The engine turns over at a moderate speed. You are waiting until the engine warms up a little. Gasoline engines run best when they are hot.

You are now ready to ride off. You seat your bike and push it forward to get it down from the kickstand. The stand snaps back and out of the way. With one foot on the ground, you hold your bike upright. Next you push the clutch lever on the left end of the handlebar against the handgrip. At the same time, you move the gear lever to first gear. You twist the throttle to give the engine more fuel. The engine speeds up. You slowly release the clutch lever and away you go. You twist the throttle grip a little more. Your machine speeds up. Now you shift into second gear. You work the clutch lever and then the gearshift lever. When you release the clutch lever, you give the engine a little more fuel. Then you shift your way up through all the gears until you are in top gear. After five minutes or so, you open the choke if it has not opened automatically already.

To slow down or stop, you grip the **hand brake** and step on the **foot brake.** The hand brake controls the front wheel and is operated by a lever on the left end of the handlebars. The foot brake controls the rear wheel and is beneath your foot. Seventy percent of a motorcycle's stopping power is in the front brake. Thus, for greatest safety, the hand brake should always be used along with the foot brake.

If you are only making a temporary stop, you also press the clutch lever and shift to neutral. This lets the motor continue to run.

## Speed

Speed depends on engine power. The harder you push a motorcycle, the faster it will go. But speed also depends on the bike's resistance to being pushed. This resistance, surprising as it may seem, is due mainly to the air through which the bike is being pushed.

Up until about 30 miles (48 km) per hour, it is mainly the weight of the motorcycle and the drag of its tires on the road that holds it back. But when the motorcycle goes faster than this, air resistance holds the bike's speed down. For example, at 100 miles (160 km) per hour, 89 percent of a bike's engine power is used up just pushing the air aside!

Since the front end of a motorcycle is small, it does not take a lot of horsepower to make a bike go fast. Incidentally, horsepower means just that—the amount of power a horse can exert when pulling. An ordinary motorcycle with a 350-cc engine can easily go better than 100 miles (160 km) per hour on a level road.

When you streamline the same motorcycle just a little, it can go more than 150 miles (240 km) per hour. Streamlining means that the motorcycle—or anything else—is tapered so that it does not catch the air. For example, a log is not streamlined. But if you cut it so that its ends are pointed, you are streamlining it. With its ends pointed the log can go through water much more easily. A fish is highly streamlined. This is why it can go through water so easily.

**Drivers trying to set speed records
lie practically flat in
their sausage-shaped motorcycles.**

When a motorcycle is perfectly or nearly perfectly streamlined, very high speeds can be reached. Motorcycles designed for speed and nothing else look like giant sausages on two wheels. The driver usually lies flat on his or her back inside the sausage. Such special motorcycles have reached speeds of over 300 miles (483 km) per hour using 350-cc engines. This same-size engine can drive a nonstreamlined bike no more than 100 miles (160 km) per hour.

## Mileage

The distance a motorcycle can go on a gallon (3.8 l) of gasoline depends on a number of things. First, there is speed. The faster the motorcycle goes, the less miles to the gallon it will get. Second, there is weight. The larger the motorcycle the heavier it is, and the less mileage it will get.

Third, there is engine size. This is something not too many people realize. A big engine doing a big job burns a lot of fuel. Everyone knows that. A big engine doing a small job wastes a lot of fuel. Not too many people know that. A driver can get much more mileage from a small engine working hard than from a large engine that is loafing.

# CHAPTER THREE

# MODERN MOTORCYCLES

Years ago, when inventors were still struggling to build the first motorcycles, they were happy if their machines just worked. As time went by, and better and better machines were built, the need for specialized machines grew. While a general-duty motorcycle is highly useful, it cannot be used for everything.

In a sense, all motorcycles manufactured today are special. Each has a special purpose. Yet, in addition, each also is either a dirt bike, a street bike, or a combination dirt and street bike.

**Street bikes.** A street bike is any motorcycle that can be legally driven over a public road. This means that the motorcycle must have license plates, a horn, turn signals, a silencer, front and rear lights, and a rearview mirror. The motorcycle can be large or small. It can be factory- or even home-built. As long as the police permit the machine to be driven over public roads, the motorcycle is called a street bike.

In addition to meeting equipment requirements, street bikes must also be powerful enough to keep up with traffic. Generally, a motorcycle made to be driven on public roads has a 125-cc or larger engine. It is not that a smaller engine will not bring you up to speed. It is that a smaller engine will take too long to get there. A small engine does not have the acceleration a large engine has. Acceleration means being able to go from slow speed to high speed quickly.

But some small engines can drive a motorcycle pretty fast. Recently a Dutchman, Henk van Kessel, pushed a motorcycle with a 50-cc engine to 137.38 miles (221.08 km) per hour.

**Dirt bikes.** Anything with two wheels that moves under its own power can be called a dirt bike. Of course, a real dirt bike

## STREET AND
## COMBINATION BIKES.

BMW R65

BMW R100RS

**HONDA CBX**

**MOTO GUZZI V1000**

**DUCATI DESMO 900**

**MOTO GUZZI 850 LEMANS**

**KAWASAKI 750**

**YAMAHA XS ELEVEN**

is made for riding on dirt—along backwoods trails and across open fields. But a dirt bike doesn't have to be made especially for dirt-riding to be called a dirt bike.

The main difference between a street bike and a dirt bike is that the dirt bike does not have the equipment that would make it legal to drive over public roads.

**Combination bikes.** Since most riders have to travel over public roads to get to the woods and other secluded areas, some motorcycles are made for both street- and dirt-riding. These combination motorcycles are usually just dirt bikes with lights, a horn, plates, and high fenders. Regular dirt bikes do not have lights, a horn, a rearview mirror, and so on because these things can get in the way when the motorcycle is going through the woods. Cyclists driving over rough ground fall off their bikes many more times than do riders motorcycling over good roads.

As we said earlier, all bikes today are made for some special purpose. Here are some of the more common "special" motorcycles.

## MINIBIKES

Any motorcycle with 14-inch (35.6-cm) or smaller wheels, an engine of less than 4 horsepower, and a seat no more than 25 inches (63.5 cm) above the ground can be considered a minibike.

Minibikes are almost always dirt bikes. They are not street-legal, and for good reason. The driver of a minibike sits so

**A Suzuki minibike, which
will go no more than about
12 miles (16 km) per hour.**

low that he or she would be very hard to see when driving between automobiles or trucks on busy streets or highways.

The first minibikes were made for use by American paratroopers during World War II. After the war, the unused machines were sold to the public. Today, a number of companies still make minibikes because so many people find them fun to ride.

Minibikes are small enough to be placed in the trunk of a car. But they have a lot of power for their size. They can easily carry a grown person across soft dirt and up and down backwoods trails.

Although minibikes are definitely dangerous on public roads and are often criticized for being poorly made, they are in at least one way safer than ordinary motorcycles. The driver sits so low to the ground that he or she cannot fall very far should there be a spill. This is why so many parents let their young children ride them.

Minibikes usually weigh less than 100 pounds (45 kg). They are not more than 60 inches (152.4 cm) long. Their engines are rarely larger than 100 cc. They almost never produce more than 4 horsepower. Minibike speeds are usually under 30 miles (48 km) per hour. This is because they are geared way down. The engine turns over fast, but the rear wheel turns slowly. This gives the minibike the pull needed to climb hills and get through sand.

One group of minibikes weigh less than 30 pounds (13.6 kg). A large watermelon weighs more. These so-called micro-cycles are so small they can fit into a suitcase.

Finally, there are the mini-cycles. These are small motorcycles that are larger than micro-cycles and other minibikes but not as large as regular motorcycles. Micro-cycles are not permitted on public roads. Some mini-cycles are.

## MOPEDS

The first moped was built by the Werner brothers in 1899. They called it a motorcyclette, but it was really a moped. The major difference between a moped and a motorcycle is pedals. A moped has pedals you can use to help the motor go up hills and to move the machine when the motor runs out of fuel.

Standard motorcycles have power trains. To start, stop, and change speed, you have to work the clutch and gearshift lever. Mopeds have automatic transmissions. They do all this for you.

You start a moped like an ordinary motorcycle. Then you just use the throttle and brake to go and stop. When you come to a very steep hill, you either help the engine by using the pedals or the moped simply stands still. The motor keeps on running.

Mopeds are basically so safe and simple to drive that some states, four to be exact, will let you drive them on most public roads no matter what age you are and without a license. However, this is changing. Moped licensing is expected to become a requirement nationwide within the next three to five years. Age and insurance requirements will also become more strict.

Mopeds weigh about 100 pounds (45 kg). They are a little smaller than a small, standard motorcycle. Their engines are very small. To qualify as a moped, the engine must be smaller than 50 cc and produce 2 horsepower or less. Moped speed is usually limited by law to 30 miles (48 km) per hour. If the machine goes faster than this, it is not a moped but a motorcycle. (Street motorcycles must meet state motorcycle road requirements. Mopeds do not have to.)

# POPULAR MOPEDS

**HONDA PA50**

**MOTOBECANE'S
VELOSOLEX**

**MOTO GUZZI'S ROBIN**

**MOTOBECANE'S
MOBYLETTE**

**HONDA EXPRESS**

**MOTOBECANE'S 7**

Moped mileage is fantastic. All mopeds will go more than 75 miles (120 km) on a gallon (3.8 l) of gas. Some will do better than 200 miles (320 km) on a gallon (3.8 l).

People in Europe and Asia have used mopeds for many years. They use them for fun or in place of cars for everyday travel. It is estimated that there are more than fifty million mopeds in daily use on these two continents alone. In the United States, however, mopeds are only now becoming popular.

## MOTORSCOOTERS

Motorscooters, like mopeds, are light in weight, not very powerful, and easy to drive. Motorscooter wheels, however, are very small, and most of the machinery is covered. This makes them comfortable to ride and relatively safe. In the United States they are used mostly for recreation.

## TRAIL BIKES

These are dirt bikes made for recreational use. They are built to handle rugged dirt roads and paths. Usually they have a single-cylinder two-stroke engine. To hold weight down, the engine is usually small—generally a 100 to a 175 cc.

## CAFE RACERS

Most cafe racers are never raced. Racing might scratch their paint. Cafe racers are designed and built for flash. Their wealth of chrome and bright shades are intended to please the eye.

## SOME POPULAR DIRT BIKES

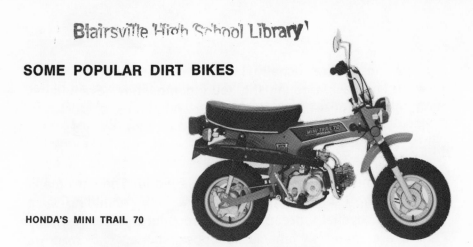

**HONDA'S MINI TRAIL 70**

**SUZUKI RM-100**

**KAWASAKI 175**

Cafe racers are usually larger than an average street bike but not as large as the touring monsters. Sometimes, though, cafe racers cost as much as touring bikes.

## CHOPPERS

These are the clowns of the motorcycle world. They are made by "chopping" standard machines apart and rebuilding them to match a cyclist's dream. Some are built by their owners. Others are made by special chopper shops. The work is highly skilled. The cost of a shop-made chopper is therefore very high.

## TOURING MOTORCYCLES

These are the Lincoln Continentals of the motorcycle world. Touring motorcycles sometimes weigh more than 600 pounds (272 kg), without fuel or rider. Their engines can be as large as 1,200 cc and have four cylinders. Some of the larger touring bikes cost more than a small car. But they are the most comfortable of all the motorcycles. If you want to go far, fast, and easy, a touring bike is the way to go.

# CHAPTER FOUR

# MOTORCYCLES IN PEACE AND WAR

## TRANSPORTATION

It is estimated that until a year or two ago, less than 5 percent of all motorcycles in the United States were being used for daily transportation. (Most of the rest were being used for fun.) Since then that figure has been increasing rapidly.

In Europe, where gasoline has always cost a lot more than it has here, motorcycles—especially mopeds with their tremendous gas mileage—have always been used more than automobiles. It is believed that out of Europe's fifty million motorcycles, 90 percent or more are used each day for transportation.

In addition to buying increasing numbers of mopeds, Americans today are buying many more small street-bikes and combination bikes than they used to.


## POLICE USE

Since early motorcycles could outrun early cars, it was only natural that police were given motorcycles to do their work. In the early 1920s, many American police rode the huge Indian Aces (no longer being manufactured). These motorcycles were just about the biggest and fastest of their time. They had four cylinders and 1,229-cc engines. The big Harley Davidsons were also popular.

The officers chosen to ride the big machines in the 1920s were equally big and strong. They had to be. They had to chase speeding cars and escaping criminals over some terrible roads in those days. Even back then, the big bikes could go better than 100 miles (160 km) per hour. To protect themselves from injury and to keep warm, the motorcycle police would wear leather puttees (leg protectors), big

**An early Indian Ace.**

leather gloves, and horsehide leather jackets. They also wore riding britches similar to those worn by the U.S. cavalry.

As the years went by, most motorcycle police were shifted to police cars. One reason was that cars became as fast as motorcycles. With high-speed cars available, it just didn't seem to make sense to purchase transportation that could be used only in good weather.

Another reason might have been the tremendous increase in road traffic. Though few actual accidents have been recorded, it certainly *looks* very dangerous to race a motorcycle down a modern and busy superhighway.

Motorcycle police have not disappeared altogether, however. In the western United States, where the weather is fair most of the year, many traffic police can still be seen mounted on motorcycles. They roar along just as they used to in the old days. But now each motorcycle has a two-way radio. Very often, the motorcycle officer is in radio contact with a helicopter. Very few law violators ever escape a motorcycle-helicopter team.

## SPECIAL DELIVERY

There used to be a time when every newspaper had its own "Dusty Roads," a daredevil young man with a motorcycle, who could outride the wind and rush a story or photograph to the newspaper editor. There was a time when young people could make money with their motorcycles delivering special-delivery letters for the post office and telegrams for Western Union. This kind of service has died out in most places. Mail carriers today use cars, and most telegrams are delivered by reading them aloud over the telephone.

In the big cities, however, there are still some messenger

services that use motorcyclists. A motorcycle can move in heavy traffic where often a car cannot. Also, in a busy city it is a lot easier to find parking space for a motorcycle than for even a small car.

## SOLDIERS ON TWO WHEELS

Though bicycles have frequently been used in war to move large companies of men from place to place, motorcycles never were. This is not as strange as it may seem. A troop of motorcycle riders would be easy to hear far away. Trucks also make noise, but they were more popular than motorcycles. A lot of soldiers could ride in one vehicle and only one of them had to know how to drive.

As early as 1875, the Italian army used bicyclists as dispatch riders, soldiers who carried messages to troops on the move. By 1885, the Belgians, French, and Austrians equipped some of their soldiers with folding bicycles. These bicycles weighed less than 28 pounds (12.7 kg). The soldiers carried them on their backs. It took them just thirty seconds to assemble the bicycles and get rolling.

In Britain in 1885, a group of soldiers were given giant-front-wheel ordinaries. The men were not expected to march. They were expected to ride their bicycles to war.

With the passing of time, the use of bicycles by the armies of the world increased. In 1907, military inventors attached two bicycles side by side with a machine gun mounted between them.

In World War I, a large number of troops rode bicycles. At the most, men on foot could do no more than 30 miles (48 km) a day, and this for not more than a few days. On a bicycle,

**Early bicycles being used by the French army.**

a soldier could easily travel 100 miles (160 km) per day, day after day. All that he needed was a hard, dry road.

During World War II, some British paratroopers carried folding bicycles with them as they jumped into enemy territory. On D day, some Canadian soldiers carried folding bicycles with them as they waded ashore.

Motorcycles were never used to move soldiers, but they were made into fighting machines. In 1899, the British army mounted a machine gun on a Simms Motor Scout. The Simms was one of the early English motorcycles.

As used by the army, however, the Simms was not a true motorcycle but a quadracycle. Two motorcycle frames were attached to a third frame. A single gasoline engine was positioned on this. The driver sat on a bicycle seat and steered both front wheels by means of a single handlebar. The machine gun was mounted near this handlebar.

This was 1899. Sixteen years would pass before a way of firing a machine gun by remote control would be invented. The driver of the Simms Motor Scout was thus at a distinct disadvantage. He had to let go of the handlebar to fire the gun —a most impractical situation!

Only a few Simms Motor Scouts were ever made. None were ever actually used in a battle.

At the start of World War I (1914) wireless, as radio was called in those days, was new. The equipment was crude and undependable. Messages could only be sent short distances and they had to be sent in Morse code—dots and dashes. You couldn't talk over the wireless, and the enemy could listen to your code messages.

There were millions of soldiers belonging to both sides spread all over Europe. The only good way of getting a secret message to the troops was to have someone carry it. Here is where the motorcycle proved its worth. Time and time again, the motorcycle dispatch rider was shown to be the fastest and most dependable of all message carriers.

By 1918, the British had more than thirty thousand motorcycles and an equal number of dispatch riders to ride them. The motorcycle used most often was the Triumph, a motorcycle that is still popular in Britain and the United States today. The American Expeditionary Force—the name given to the American army overseas, had about ten thousand Indians and a significant number of Harley Davidsons. The Germans relied mainly on NSU (Neckarsulm Verke) motorcycles.

During this period an effort was made to replace the British cavalry with motorcyclists. A sidecar was attached to each motorcycle. A machine gun and a second rider were placed in each sidecar. The idea was that one person would drive the motorcycle. The other would be free to fire the machine gun. It was believed that together the two soldiers and the machine gun would be more effective than a single soldier on horseback. It didn't prove to be that way. The armored motorcycles and their sidecars were soon taken out of service.

Strangely enough, some fifteen hundred of these motorcycles found their way to Russia after World War I was over.

As radio improved, the need for dispatch riders decreased. At the start of World War II, the U.S. army had only some thirty-five hundred motorcycles on hand. Their numbers diminished even further as the war progressed.

The Germans during World War II relied much more heavily on motorcycles than did the Allies. Actually, at the outbreak of the war the United States had been planning to make the motorcycle a mainstay of military transportation, especially

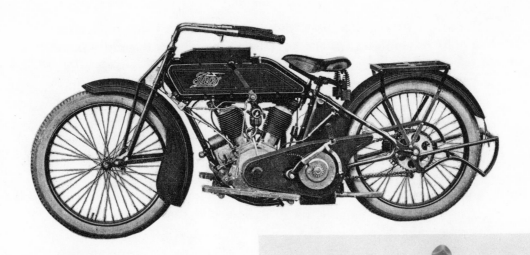

Above: an early motorcycle developed for military use. Right: two doughboys from World War I riding a Harley-Davidson motorcycle with a sidecar.

A later version of the motorcycle sidecar, on display at the 1939 World's Fair.

**Above: a 1939 British motorcyclist division. Left: an American motorcycle messenger in Germany in 1944. Right: World War II dispatch riders in France.**

in the European theatre. But before the plan could be carried out, the jeep was developed. The Germans didn't have the jeep.

Most of the German motorcycles were very similar to those used by the British and Americans at the time. There was one exception. The Germans had a giant motorcycle. In front it had a single, extra-large wheel, just like a standard motorcycle. The wheel was turned by the handlebars. The driver sat on a standard seat behind the middle of the handlebars. There was no single wheel behind the driver. Instead, there were a pair of caterpillar treads like those used on military tanks and bulldozers. The purpose of the treads was to enable the giant motorcycle to cross soft mud and ditches.

The giant motorcycle probably did not work very well. Only a few were built.

The men and more than a few women who rode motorcycles in World War II must have found it both exciting and scary. There were very few good roads. Most were covered with shell holes, broken concrete, and mud. What the enemy did not do with their big guns and bombs, the armies did. A modern army with half a million soldiers and thousands of vehicles of all kinds can take a week to pass a given point. When the army has passed, what was a smooth, thick concrete road is dust and mud.

Also, in some areas there were no road lights. To provide some light on a moonless night, soldiers in the area would shine giant searchlights up at the clouds. The light that was reflected back down wasn't as bright as the light from a full moon, but it was better than nothing. This light was called artificial moonlight.

Most of the time neither side shot directly at dispatch

riders. They were too small and unimportant. But every now and again a lone plane would chase a motorcycle dispatch rider across the landscape. Sometimes the pilot would do so because he had been told the rider carried a very important dispatch. Sometimes the pilot chased the motorcycle rider simply because the rider was the enemy and the pilot had nothing better to do.

These are just a few examples of the dangers motorcycle dispatch riders on both sides had to contend with during the war.

# CHAPTER FIVE

# RACING AND OTHER FORMS OF MOTORCYCLE COMPETITION

Humans have always liked to race. In prehistoric days, people raced on foot, horseback, even camelback. After the wheel was invented some six thousand years ago, men raced in two-wheel wagons called chariots. All the early peoples raced chariots, including the Egyptians, Greeks, and Romans. Chariots were pulled by one, two, three, or even four horses. The more horsepower, the faster the chariot went.

The first bicycles, the Celeriferes, were raced down the avenues of Paris. The first cars were raced in Britain, France, Germany—wherever there were two or more cars in one place.

At first, drivers raced their machines whenever they got together and felt like racing. But before very long, clubs were formed. Prizes were awarded by the clubs, by rich individuals, and by companies.

Vehicle manufacturers soon learned the value of winning races. The public liked speed. Makes of vehicles that won races sold the best. So manufacturers made racing their business. It is still their business today.

Manufacturers also soon learned that racing was a quick and reliable way to test their machines.

At first the prizes won in races were small. Racing drivers and mechanics were paid little by the companies who hired them to drive. In the early years, around 1900, driving a winning machine meant much more glory and satisfaction than money.

Today, the driver of a winning car at the Indianapolis 500, for example, can expect to earn a million dollars. Part of this is prize money. The rest comes from the winner getting a chance to participate in the advertising and promotion of products.

Motorcycle racing does not pay this well. The largest single prize in motorcycle competition is only $50,000. It is not for motorcycle racing. It is for motorcycle jumping (more about jumping later).

## PRIVATEERS AND
## FACTORY RIDERS

Modern motorcycle competition differs from modern car racing in that most motorcycle racers are privateers. They own their own machines, pay their own way, and race for their own fun and profit. They do not race for a manufacturer or factory.

Car racing is just the opposite. Most car race drivers belong to a factory team. Few own or drive their own race cars.

The reason is money. It may take a million dollars to put a car in a big race. Any machine will not do. The car must have a chance of winning or it will not even be allowed to enter. A Formula 1 racer (Formula means it must be built according to certain rules), for example, can cost a quarter of a million dollars. And one racing car is not enough. Very often a racing driver will smash the first car during practice or the engine will burn out. Without a second and even a third car standing by, and lots of spare parts, a driver can be out of a race even before he or she starts.

A single driver cannot win any big race. Cars do not carry enough gas to finish the race. They must stop for fuel, tire changes, and sometimes repairs. These are called pit stops. Pit stops are part of the race. To cut pit stops short, a trained crew stand ready. They do things in minutes that the driver alone could not do in an hour.

The extra racing cars, the crew, the extra parts, the training and travel—all these things add up to a great deal of money.

Stock car racing is a little different. This is where you will find some owner-drivers. A stock car is an everyday car that can be bought at any showroom. Some changes are allowed and made, but not many. Stock cars can be driven down the public highway. Formula 1 cars and other special racing cars cannot. They must be carried on the back of a truck or in a plane.

Motorcycle racing is very different. As said earlier, most of the drivers are privateers. They own their own machines. They race for themselves. There aren't many factory riders in motorcycle competition. But factory riders win most of the big races and prizes. Why this is will be explained shortly.

The cost of a top-quality motorcycle good enough to be driven in stiff competition is very low compared to that of a racing car. The cost of racing motorcycles is kept low by means of claiming races.

A claiming race is an ordinary race. But after it is over, the winning motorcycle must be put up for sale. And, according to claiming-race rules, it cannot be sold for more than $7,500. If more than one person bids (makes an offer) for the winning motorcycle, a drawing is held. The winner of the drawing gets to buy the motorcycle.

Even if a factory spends more than $7,500 to build its motorcycle, it must sell it for no more than $7,500 if it wins. All the money spent over this sum is lost. In this way the cost of racing motorcycles is held down.

There are three reasons why factory riders win most of the big prizes and races. First of all, when a privateer begins to win a lot of races, a factory will offer him or her a job to ride for them. Since the factory can guarantee the rider perhaps $100,000 to $150,000 for a year's riding, few privateers turn the offer down.

The second reason is again money. Few privateers can afford to travel the big circuits. It costs a lot to haul one or two motorcycles around the world. Travel expenses and entry fees must usually be paid before the race. So unless a privateer has lots of money beforehand, he or she cannot even get started.

Most privateers haul their bikes behind their cars on a trailer. They camp out for a night or two when they have to. This lets them attend races some distance from their home. But they cannot get away so cheaply for international competitions.

Still another reason why the factory riders win the big ones is engineering. Most racing bikes begin as standard or stock machines. But winning bikes are usually altered a dozen ways to make them run and handle better.

Here privateers sometimes have the edge over the factory riders. Some privateers know and understand motorcycle engines far better than most factory engineers do. But the factories have the big machine shops—test benches and test equipment. It is very difficult to make major engine changes without the proper tools and equipment.

All kinds of engine changes are made. Sometimes the valves are made larger. Sometimes larger carburetors are used. Sometimes the inlet and exhaust pipes are made smoother on the inside. Sometimes larger pipes are used.

No single change turns a standard engine into a racing engine. A lot of small changes are needed. No matter how smart the privateer may be, he or she is not going to improve an engine with just a touch here and an adjustment there.

The more power a motorcycle engine has, the more chance the rider has of that bike winning. That is why racing drivers will make as many changes in their engines as they dare. Many times they ask too much of their engines. They change them too much, force them too far. This is why so many motorcycle (and car) engines break down in the middle of a race.

## Riders Count As
## Much As Machines

The best machines do not always win. A lot depends on the rider. Motorcycle racing takes a lot of skill, strength, and daring. Most winning motorcycle racers are twenty-three or twenty-four years old. Only a very few are over thirty. (On an average, car racing drivers are ten years older than motorcycle racing drivers.)

Factories go out of their way to find and hire young drivers. As the "hired hands" get older and perhaps wiser, they become more cautious. They take fewer chances. They do not win as often as younger riders. And so they are replaced.

Many riders, especially those who are willing to take great risks, are injured. A few have even been killed. Professional motorcycle and car racing are really dangerous sports.

## MOTORCYCLE
## COMPETITIONS

Car drivers race against each other and against time. They race in large and small cars, on paved roads, and on dirt

**A number of competition riders, particularly the
winners, work for manufacturers. Here, Jim Rice,
who leads the pack, is representing Harley-Davidson.**

**Observed trials include some really rough terrain.
Here the rider is on a Bultaco, a specially
designed trials bike manufactured in Spain.**

roads. Motorcyclists do the same, but they also compete in observed trials, enduros, motocross, cross-country scrambles, TT scrambles, ISD races, sidecar racing, hill climbing, endurance racing, motorcycle jumping, and speed trials.

## Observed Trials

Have you ever watched a motorcyclist drive through water or mud 2 feet (.6 m) deep, climb over boulders 7 feet (2.1 m) high, jump fallen logs and ditches, or drive down the length of a log stretched across a creek? If you have, then you have witnessed observed trials.

No one knows exactly when the sport of observed trials began. Most likely it started with some cyclists showing off their bike-handling ability. In just the last few years observed trials have grown tremendously. Today it is an international sport. There are thousands of riders competing. There are observed-trials clubs. There are even schools that teach riders how to ride and win in these contests.

There is now an Observed Trials World Championship Series. It consists of twelve contests. One is held in the United States. The winner of the series has his or her name put on the Wagner Cup.

The reason for all this enthusiasm is mainly that winning depends on judgment, good balancing skill, and a feel for the machine. It does not depend on brute strength and stamina. Observed trials are not really dangerous. Contestants wear lightweight, bicycle-type helmets.

To win an observed-trials contest, a rider must guide his or her machine over rough stretches of earth and water without stopping or losing control.

Each stretch of ground is called a section. There may be ten to twenty sections, each 10 to 100 feet (3 to 30 m) long.

The section may be straight or it may have turns. The sides of the section are clearly marked with poles and flags or string.

The rider may enter a section or trap, as it is often called, whenever he or she wishes. He or she may ride as fast or as slowly as desired. Time inside the section is not measured.

Once inside a section the rider must leave by its marked exit. At no time can the rider come to a full stop. Neither can the rider go off course or leave the section before reaching its exit. To do either costs the rider five points. To put a foot on the ground, called dabbing, costs the rider one point. But no matter how often the rider loses control, he or she is never penalized more than eight points in any one section.

When the rider leaves a section, he or she may rest and examine the following section. Anything that goes on between sections does not count. Riders can walk their machines from one section to another if they wish. Or they can ride from section to section.

Usually a large scorecard is fastened to the front of each motorcycle. When a rider leaves one section, the judge or judges mark the score on cards for all to see. In this way spectators can keep track of how well the riders are doing.

Spectators are silent while a contestant is within a section. They do not want to disturb the rider's concentration. They applaud only after the contestant has completed the section.

The reason for this is the nature of the traps. They are really tough.

The seventh round of the 1978 Observed Trials World Championship Series was held in the United States in Roaring Branch Motorsport Park deep in the Pennsylvania mountains. Together, the nineteen sections and the open spaces between them stretched some 8 miles (12.9 km). Most of the sections

The observed trials contestant in this picture failed to go between the flags and so will be penalized. The bike being ridden is an Ossa, another Spanish-built model.

**The contestant in this enduro
race is fording a small stream.**

were at the bottom of Cascade Run. This is a mountain stream with hundreds of waterfalls. In many places the stream appeared to be impassable.

All the riders walked each section three and four times to get themselves ready. The bottom of Cascade Run was water-polished rock. In some places this rock was covered by slippery moss.

But the mountain stream wasn't the only problem. Some of the sections went straight up muddy hillsides. Most of the sections were 400 yards (366 m) long.

Most serious trial riders use 250-cc single-cylinder two-stroke bikes made especially for trials by three Spanish companies—Bultaco, Montessa, and Ossa.

## Enduro Racing

Contestants often claim that enduros are simply trials that go on forever. There is some truth in what they say. An enduro run can stretch 250 miles (402 km). The course the racers have to follow may take them through deserts, mountains, forest paths, shallow water, swamps, or even jungles.

Speed does not count in a trials contest. But it does count in an enduro. Not top speed, but a special speed.

Like trials, enduros are divided into sections. Each section is usually between 10 and 15 miles (16 and 24 km) long and calls for its own speed. This speed can be anything from 10 to 30 miles (16 to 48 km) per hour. Each rider tries to hold as closely to the posted speed as possible. Going more slowly or more quickly loses the rider points.

There are observers all along the path the racers must follow. The observers check the racer's speed. Riders cannot win by speeding up when the going is easy and slowing down when the going gets tough. They must hold closely to the required speed to win. As you can imagine, this is not easy. Hence the name of the race: enduro, for endurance.

To make enduros fair, contestants are divided into classes or groups according to the engine size of the machines they ride. Inexperienced riders usually compete on 100-cc machines. The more experienced riders use anything up to 350-cc machines. Almost all motorcycles built for enduro contests have single-cylinder two-stroke engines. Like trials motorcycles they are designed for lightness, power, and easy handling.

## Motocross Racing

Until recently, motocross (MX) racing was the name some European cyclists gave to enduro racing. Motocross racing is a kind of endurance contest. However it has never had any real historical connection to enduro racing.

Motocross racing is a head-to-head race on rough ground. All cyclists start at the same time. The first to finish a certain distance or a number of laps wins. Sometimes the race will be limited to a certain number of minutes. The rider going farthest in the given time wins.

Generally there isn't one race but two or three heats or short races called motos. Each moto may be ten to forty minutes long. To win, a rider must finish each moto and must do better than anyone else. But he or she doesn't have to win all the motos. For example, a rider can win the contest by taking one first place and two second places, provided no one else has two first places.

Since cycles with bigger engines go faster, motocross racing is divided into classes by engine size. One class is limited to cycles having engines no larger than 125 cc. Another class is limited to 250-cc engines, and there is a third class limited to 500-cc engines.

Motocross racing is now big-time. There is a series of world championship MX races held every year in Europe and the United States called the Grand Prix ("large prize"). In addition, the United States has its own motocross series known as the Nationals.

All these races are well attended. Thirty or forty thousand spectators and a hundred or more riders are not unusual. Many MX races can be seen on television.

Recently, MX racing went indoors. Thousands of tons of dirt were hauled into the New Orleans Superdome. A tough, rough, bumpy dirt track was set up. Forty thousand spectators showed up to cheer the riders on.

Motocross racing is the most difficult and dangerous form of motorcycle racing. Riders can at times achieve speeds of more than 80 miles (129 km) per hour, but the course is laid out in such a rough, curvy fashion that average speed is kept to about 30 miles (48 km) per hour. The track is usually between one-half and a mile and one-half (.8 and 2.4 km) long. Some tracks include 4-foot- (1.2-m) wide jumps. None of the tracks is paved. They are all soft dirt. This frequently causes cycles to slide and skid out of control. It is no wonder that MX racing chews up riders and machines faster than any other form of motorcycle racing.

## Cross-Country
## Scrambles

This is a fun race. Sometimes it is called a hare-and-hounds scramble. Someone who is not going to race rides cross-country and lays out a route. He or she will set flagpoles into

81)

the ground. The racers in the contest all start out at the same time. The cyclist who reaches the last marker wins. Since none of the racers know where the flagpoles are, it is a scramble. The rider who leads has the job of finding the markers. The dust eaters, those who follow, do not have this problem. They just follow the cloud of dust. If the leader of the pack makes an error and goes the wrong way, a slower but wiser cyclist can win the race.

## TT Scrambles

When British road laws prohibited motorcyclists from going faster than a person could walk, motorcycle enthusiasts went to the Isle of Man in the Irish Sea to race. Since the British were tourists there, they named the trophy for which they raced the Tourist Trophy (TT).

The best riders in the world now compete every year in the races held on the foggy and rainy Isle of Man. In 1978, some ten thousand riders and spectators came to the island, which normally has less than fifty-five thousand inhabitants.

The TT track is about 37 miles (60 km) long, and riders often report that the fog is so thick they cannot see more than a dozen yards (11 m) ahead of them. Of course, if the fog is too bad, the race is stopped. The average course speed in good visibility is around 110 miles (177 km) per hour, but at some points racers hit 140 miles (225 km) per hour. The track includes at least one jump. The hills are so steep it is necessary to shift gears frequently.

## ISDT Races

The International Six Day Trials is often called the Olympics of motorcycle racing because it is considered the greatest single test of racing skill.

**This driver is competing in an ISDT race.**

The racers form teams of six riders each, which compete against each other for five consecutive days. The competition includes eleven events. These events are a combination of trials and enduro. The course is very, very tough, and speed counts.

On the sixth day the teams compete in all-out speed events.

## Sidecar Racing

Originally, the sidecar on a motorcycle was just that: a little, enclosed seat at the side of the motorcycle. But that didn't allow top speed. So the first major change in sidecar racing was to have the sidecar passenger kneel. Kneeling results in less air resistance. Thus the sidecar would go faster. The kneeling change was introduced back in 1954.

Today, a racing sidecar motorcycle doesn't look much like a motorcycle with a sidecar. Today it looks like a small, low car with two small wheels in front and one in the rear.

The sidecar rider has an important job to do in a race—lean out to the side to keep the sidecar from turning over when the motorcycle makes a sharp turn.

Years ago, motorcycles with sidecars could barely go 100 miles (160 km) per hour. Today they go 124 miles (200 km) per hour. Years ago, people raced sidecar motorcycles for fun. Now they are raced for prizes and trophies.

## Endurance Racing

An endurance race is run on a paved track. It is called endurance because it usually lasts two, four, six, eight hours, or even longer. The shorter races are often limited to single riders. The longer races allow two riders to share the riding time. The individual or team that goes farthest wins.

This may not seem tough, but endurance races continue through rain, snow, or fog. As the miles and hours grind on, both riders and machines get tired and break down. Competition is very tough.

At a recent six-hour endurance race held in southern California, there were five hours of steady rain. One hundred and one teams entered. The winner led the others by only eight seconds.

## Jumping Contests

Maybe Evel Knievel started it. Evel is the man who tried to jump a rocket-powered motorcycle across Snake River Canyon in Idaho in September 1974. He didn't make it. His parachute opened too soon.

Anyway, jumping motorcycles is now a profitable sport. Jumpers lift their cycles as much as 110 feet (34 m). They fly through the air with control and grace and they land on or near a target.

The winner in these contests is selected on the basis of takeoff control, control and posture going through the air, and on how close the rider comes to a small square painted on the landing ramp.

The jump consists of a takeoff ramp, an obstacle of some twenty or so cars placed side by side, and a landing ramp. The trick to landing on target is to control takeoff speed. A fraction faster or slower than calculated results in missing the target.

Contest prize money is high. A recent world championship of motorcycle jumping paid $50,000 in cash prizes with $20,000 going to the winner.

Another $5,000 was offered to any rider who would jump

**This is really part of a hill-climbing event,
though it looks more like jumping. The rider
in the picture is about to cross the finish line.**

twenty cars for a distance of 120 feet (37 m) to establish a new world record. The present record is 117 feet (35.6 m). Bob Duffy, who is in his thirties and has done a lot of stunt work, tried it. He made the distance but landed on one wheel, skidding and shaking himself up. The jump didn't count because he didn't make a clean landing. He wasn't hurt, but he didn't try again.

## Hill Climbing

Not only does the rider have to get to the top of a steep hill without falling to win, he or she has to do so in less time than any other rider.

Many cyclists believe that hill climbing may have been the first clocked cycle competition. Clocked means that the time it takes to do something is measured with a stopwatch.

The most famous hill climb takes place each year at Mount Garfield. This is a steep, 320-foot (98-m) hill just outside of Muskegon, Michigan.

## Speed Trials

These all-out attempts to shatter world speed records for various kinds and types of motorcycles are run each year on the Bonneville salt flats in Utah. The flats are the dried-up bottom of an ancient lake. The surface is hard and perfectly flat.

Each cycle is permitted to travel as far as its driver wishes in order to get up speed. Then the cycle's speed is measured over a distance of exactly one mile (1.6 km).

The world's motorcycle speed record is 318.5 miles (512.6 km) per hour. It was set by Don Vesco in August 1978. He rode a sausage-shaped motorcycle 21 feet (6.4 m) long.

# INDEX